The Peaceful Pencil

COLOURING
MEDITATION

75 MINDFUL PATTERNS TO ENJOY

PEONY PRESS

Relax and unwind with this stress-relieving colouring book of mindful mandalas. The art of colouring is a form of meditation, focusing the mind and stilling the endless mental chatter that saps our energy and causes stress and negative feelings. As you start to colour in these mandalas you will unleash your inner creativity and find yourself gradually moving to a more peaceful and calming state of mind.

You can colour in as little or as much as you like, taking your time to develop your picture the way you want it. There are no hard and fast rules, you are truly free to create your own unique designs whether you choose pencils, pens or paints. Start colouring today and enjoy the still, quiet voice of calm this soothing practice will bring you.

EVERYTHING THAT SLOWS US DOWN AND FORCES
PATIENCE, EVERYTHING THAT SETS US BACK INTO
THE SLOW CIRCLES OF NATURE, IS A HELP.

MAY SARTON

THE SECRET OF HEALTH FOR BOTH MIND AND BODY
IS NOT TO MOURN FOR THE PAST, NOR TO WORRY
ABOUT THE FUTURE, BUT TO LIVE THE PRESENT
MOMENT WISELY AND EARNESTLY.

BUDDHA

WHAT LIES BEHIND US AND WHAT LIES
BEFORE US ARE TINY MATTERS COMPARED TO
WHAT LIES WITHIN US.

RALPH WALDO EMERSON

INNER PEACE IS IMPOSSIBLE WITHOUT PATIENCE.
WISDOM REQUIRES PATIENCE. SPIRITUAL GROWTH
IMPLIES THE MASTERY OF PATIENCE. PATIENCE
ALLOWS THE UNFOLDING OF DESTINY TO
PROCEED AT ITS OWN UNHURRIED PACE.

BRIAN WEISS

MINDFULNESS IS ABOUT BEING FULLY AWAKE
IN OUR LIVES. IT IS ABOUT PERCEIVING THE
EXQUISITE VIVIDNESS OF EACH MOMENT. WE
ALSO GAIN IMMEDIATE ACCESS TO OUR OWN
POWERFUL INNER RESOURCES FOR INSIGHT,
TRANSFORMATION, AND HEALING.

JON KABAT-ZINN

IT IS NEITHER WEALTH OR SPLENDOR,
BUT TRANQUILLITY AND OCCUPATION,
WHICH GIVE HAPPINESS.

THOMAS JEFFERSON

PRESENCE IS WHEN YOU'RE NO LONGER WAITING
FOR THE NEXT MOMENT, BELIEVING THAT THE NEXT
MOMENT WILL BE MORE FULFILLING THAN THIS ONE.

ECKHART TOLLE

BE GENTLE WITH YOURSELF. YOU ARE A CHILD
OF THE UNIVERSE, NO LESS THAN THE TREES AND
THE STARS. IN THE NOISY CONFUSION OF LIFE,
KEEP PEACE IN YOUR SOUL.

MAX EHRMANN

DON'T SEEK, DON'T SEARCH, DON'T ASK, DON'T
KNOCK, DON'T DEMAND – RELAX. IF YOU RELAX,
IT COMES. IF YOU RELAX, IT IS THERE. IF YOU RELAX,
YOU START VIBRATING WITH IT.

OSHO

THE POOR LONG FOR RICHES AND THE
RICH FOR HEAVEN, BUT THE WISE LONG FOR
A STATE OF TRANQUILLITY.

SWAMI RAMA

DISCOVER YOUR DEEP INNER SELF AND FROM
THAT PLACE SPREAD LOVE IN EVERY DIRECTION.

AMIT RAY

I AM CONTENT; THAT IS A BLESSING GREATER
THAN RICHES; AND HE TO WHOM THAT IS
GIVEN NEED ASK NO MORE.

HENRY FIELDING

OUR GREATEST WEAPON AGAINST STRESS IS OUR
ABILITY TO CHOOSE ONE THOUGHT OVER ANOTHER.

WILLIAM JAMES

THE BEST AND SAFEST THING IS TO KEEP BALANCE
IN YOUR LIFE, ACKNOWLEDGE THE GREAT POWERS
AROUND US AND IN US. IF YOU CAN DO THAT, AND
LIVE THAT WAY, YOU ARE REALLY A WISE MAN.

EURIPIDES

ONE MAN PRACTICING KINDNESS IN
THE WILDERNESS IS WORTH ALL THE TEMPLES
THIS WORLD PULLS.

JACK KEROUAC

CONTINUITY OF THOUGHT UPON ONE SINGLE
THING AND THE SUPPRESSION OF EVERY SOURCE OF
DISTRACTION MULTIPLY IN AN EXTRAORDINARY
WAY THE VALUE OF TIME.

ANONYMOUS

MOST OF US TAKE FOR GRANTED THAT
TIME FLIES, MEANING THAT IT PASSES TOO QUICKLY.
BUT IN THE MINDFUL STATE, TIME DOESN'T REALLY
PASS AT ALL. THERE IS ONLY A SINGLE INSTANT
OF TIME THAT KEEPS RENEWING ITSELF OVER
AND OVER WITH INFINITE VARIETY.

DEEPAK CHOPRA

LEARN THE RICHNESS OF SOLITUDE AND
QUIET. THAT "STILL SMALL VOICE" IS
YEARNING TO BE HEARD.

SUSAN JEFFERS

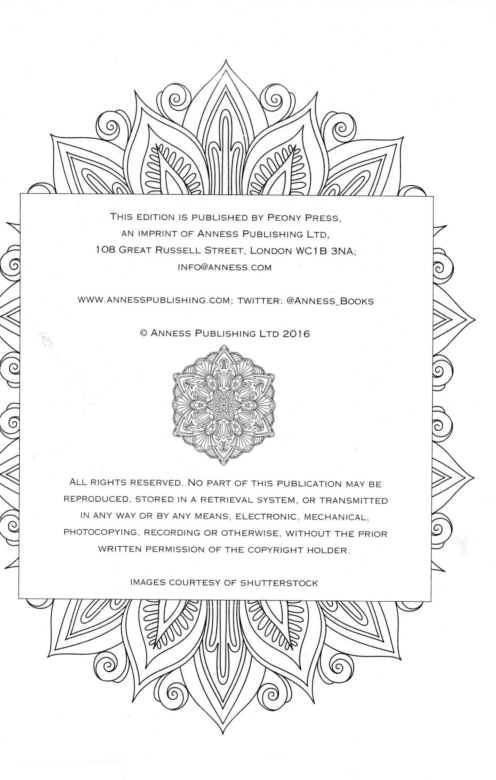

THIS EDITION IS PUBLISHED BY PEONY PRESS,
AN IMPRINT OF ANNESS PUBLISHING LTD,
108 GREAT RUSSELL STREET, LONDON WC1B 3NA;
INFO@ANNESS.COM

WWW.ANNESSPUBLISHING.COM; TWITTER: @ANNESS_BOOKS